MIRABILE: THE TRAVELER'S VIEWFINDER

DR. MAHESH PILLAI

INDIA • SINGAPORE • MALAYSIA

ISBN 979-8-89588-612-0

This book is dedicated to: My Wife Soumia and our kids, Sreeram & Durga

"In the tapestry of life, family is the most precious thread that weaves our story together. To my beloved wife Soumia Mahesh and our cherished children, Sreeram and Durga, this book is a testament to the love, strength, and enduring bonds that have enriched our lives. May these pages forever remind us of the beauty and warmth of our journey together."

Contents

Introduction

An Invitation to Wander

Welcome to a journey that transcends borders, cultures, and time zones—right from the comfort of your reading chair. Whether you're a seasoned traveler or someone yearning for new horizons, this book will ignite your spirit of adventure.

Travel is more than just moving from one place to another. It's about the connections we make, the lessons we learn, and the memories that shape us. I've traversed bustling cities, serene landscapes, and everything in between, and with every trip, I've come away not just with photos, but with stories—stories that have transformed how I see the world.

This book is an invitation to wander through the hidden alleyways of Istanbul, to stand in awe before the majestic beauty of Lake Como, to feel the vibrancy of New Orleans' jazz-filled streets, and to discover the history and culture behind every corner of Lisbon. It's about more than just checking places off a list—it's about discovering the soul of each destination.

Have you ever wondered what it feels like to truly connect with a place and its people? To step off the beaten path and into the heart of a culture? That's what this book is about—those moments of serendipity, the chance encounters, the unexpected flavors that linger long after the trip is over.

In these pages, you'll find more than just travel tales—you'll find a guide to seeing the world with fresh eyes. Whether you're planning your next trip or simply dreaming of distant lands, this book is your compass, pointing you toward deeper, richer experiences. I'll share my triumphs and mishaps, the laughter and the lessons, hoping you'll find inspiration to pack your bags or, at the very least, broaden your perspective.

So, are you ready? Adventure is calling, and the world is waiting. Let this book be your starting point—because every great journey begins with a single step, or in this case, a single page.

Let's explore together. Your next great adventure starts here.

CHAPTER I

Saving a Life at 30,000 Feet: My Experience of Helping a Passenger with an Asthma Attack

During a weekend in 2018, my wife, son, and I embarked on a trip from Riyadh, Saudi Arabia to Bahrain with the intention of spending two days there to unwind ourselves from our busy work schedules. The journey involved a five-hour drive. While enroute, I took the opportunity to call my parents in India and informed them about our trip to Bahrain and mentioned that I would be unable to communicate with them for the next couple of days as I would be occupied in Bahrain

Upon arriving in Bahrain at approximately 9:00 PM, we proceeded to check into the Bahrain International Hotel, which we had previously reserved through booking.com. After freshening up, we decided to head out to a South Indian restaurant to indulge in some of our favorite dishes. This was one of the highlights of our trip, as we always look forward to enjoying the unique flavors of South Indian cuisine whenever we travel to Bahrain.

The following morning, at around 6:00 AM, my sister called me with the heartbreaking news that my father had passed away. He had suffered a Cardiac arrest and had not woke up from his sleep. I was completely taken aback by the news, as I had spoken to him just a few hours ago and had no indication that he was unwell. He had always been healthy, and I never expected him to leave us so soon.

In my state of shock and grief, I reached out to my cousins who have been living and working in Bahrain at that time.

They arrived promptly and provided comfort and support to me and my family. They also assisted in arranging flights for us on the same day, in the afternoon, to Cochin so that we could begin making arrangements for my father's funeral. I will always be grateful for their help during this difficult time.

The passing away of my father had left me feeling deeply saddened and depressed, as he had been a constant source of motivation and support in my life. Our daily conversations, which lasted for at least an hour, were an essential part of my routine, and it was difficult to come to terms with the fact that I would no longer be able to have them. Accepting this reality was a significant challenge for me, and it took time to process my grief.

As we boarded the flight, I closed my eyes, unsure of how I would cope with the situation or what I could possibly say to my mother about the loss of my father. The upcoming days would be difficult, and I was struggling to come to terms with the reality of his sudden demise.

Approximately after an hour, an announcement was made in the cabin requesting the presence of any available doctors to report to the cabin crew. As I was not a medical doctor, I remained seated. However, I observed that no one seemed to be responding to the announcement. Being a certified first aid instructor, I approached the cabin crew and offered my assistance in case it was required.

Upon offering my assistance, the cabin crew asked me to come to the back of the cabin where there was a passenger experiencing an asthma attack. Using my training as a first aid instructor, I was able to recognize the symptoms of asthma based on the passenger's labored breathing, wheezing, and persistent dry cough.

I asked the passenger if he had an inhaler with him, but he replied that he did not. When I inquired further, he mentioned that he had not experienced an asthma attack before. As a first aid instructor, I had taught my students that in case of a first-time asthma attack, it is essential to call for emergency medical assistance. However, given that we were in an airplane, and I was the only available medical assistance, I had to rely on my training and knowledge to provide the best possible care to the passenger.

Despite providing the passenger with emergency oxygen, he did not show any improvement in his condition. In the cabin, I noticed that there were several women present, and I assumed that some of them might be nurses. However, to my surprise, none of them offered to help. While I had only received basic first aid training, these nurses would have had more extensive hands-on experience in treating patients.

It was disheartening to see that they were unwilling to assist even though the passenger's life was potentially at risk. This made me reflect on why some people might be hesitant to help in such situations, even when they have the skills and knowledge to do so.

Despite administering emergency oxygen, the passenger's condition did not improve. However, at that moment, a lady who identified herself as a nurse offered to assist me. She approached the cabin crew and requested them to make an announcement asking whether any passengers had an inhaler available. A young lady came forward with a Ventolin inhaler, which the nurse then provided to the passenger. Unfortunately, even after using the inhaler, there was no improvement in his condition.

With approximately 3 and a half hours remaining until we reached Cochin, I came to the realization that the passenger's condition was so severe that he was unlikely to survive until we reached our destination.

I approached the cabin crew and expressed my concern that the passenger might not survive until we reached Cochin. They then consulted with the captain, who joined us to discuss the situation. I informed the captain that the passenger's condition was critical and that I did not believe he would survive for the next few more hours. The captain asked me to confirm my assessment, and once I did, he suggested that we land in Muscat to seek medical assistance.

Despite my concerns, some of the people seated near the passenger attempted to reassure me, insisting that there was no need to land in Muscat and that everything would be fine. I found their reaction frustrating, as they were aware that diverting the flight to Muscat would cause delays. It seemed that their desire to reach their destination was more important to them than the life of a fellow passenger.

This experience left me feeling saddened and disappointed in human behavior. If we cannot take care of one another in such critical situations, then who will?

I ignored the objections of some passengers, I persisted in my request to the captain and he decided to land in Muscat for the sake of the critically ill passenger. We eventually landed in Muscat, and the passenger was immediately taken to the airport emergency clinic. Unfortunately, his condition did not improve, and he had to be transferred to the main hospital. Later on, we came to know that his condition was stabilized.

Although being in a state of mourning, I felt a sense of satisfaction knowing that I had played a pivotal role in saving the life of a fellow human being. Although our flight was delayed by almost three hours, and my family was eagerly waiting for me to return home to take part in my father's cremation ceremony, I knew that I had made the right decision.

Upon reaching home, my worried mother was waiting for me. I explained the situation with the passenger on the flight and the reason for our delay. Thankfully, she understood the gravity of the situation and commended me for making the right choice.

Even now, I find it difficult to understand why the nurses on board were unwilling to assist the critically ill passenger and why some passengers objected an emergency landing in Muscat. It is a sobering reminder that if we, as human beings, do not take care of one another, then who will?

I urge anyone reading this to keep in mind the importance of helping others in need. Your actions could make a significant difference and save someone's life, bringing relief not only to them but also to their loved ones. The person I assisted on the flight was a stranger to me, and yet I will always remember his face and how contented I feel to have been able to help him.

I am grateful to the cabin crew, the nurse who supported me, the young lady who provided the inhaler, the captain who made the right decision to land in Muscat, the emergency crew who evacuated the passenger from the aircraft, and the medical professionals who treated him in the airport clinic and hospital. Together, we were able to save his life that day.

Once again, I urge everyone to extend a helping hand if someone is in need. Your timely support could make a world of difference to someone in distress.

CHAPTER II

The Broken Mirror...Shattered Images of People with Hardened Boundaries of Partition

We all felt the pain and suffering of those people, and I stopped my video recording…

In 2019, I traveled to San Diego for a conference, with a few extra days to explore the city. As I scrolled through Airbnb experiences, something caught my eye—a tour to Tijuana, Mexico, led by a guide named Ricardo. The idea stirred something deep within me. Mexico had always been a dream destination, yet the media's grim reports of safety issues had kept me hesitant. But I've learned not to trust the media blindly; reality is often painted with more kindness than we're led to believe. So, I took a leap of faith and booked the tour.

Tijuana, a border city just south of San Diego, has a reputation for its vibrant culture, mouthwatering food, and buzzing nightlife. I had no idea that beyond this lively atmosphere, I would encounter something far more profound—an experience that would change the way I see borders, and the invisible lines that divide humanity.

On the morning of the tour, we met Ricardo at the U.S.-Mexico border. Besides me, there was a Canadian lady and another person from the U.S. Ricardo drove us to the crossing, but advised us to walk across—traffic could trap us for hours otherwise. I remember how quick and almost casual the border crossing was. Once we reached the Mexican side, Ricardo's driver was waiting for us.

Our first stop was the border fence—an imposing structure that stretched for miles, marking the hard line between two worlds. It was built in the 1990s to curb illegal immigration and drug trafficking, but the reality of what it symbolized was far more tragic. There were tourists taking photos, snacking at makeshift stalls. I joined them, taking pictures and absorbing the atmosphere, but something felt off.

Ricardo then told us we were going to witness something far more intimate—the emotional meetings of families separated by the border. With my camera in hand, I was eager to capture the rawness of these reunions—family members reaching through the metal bars of the fence to touch fingertips, their eyes brimming with tears and unspoken words. But then Ricardo gently advised me: "Don't capture their faces. This is too personal. It's not right to record their pain."

In that moment, I felt something break inside me. Here I was, ready to turn someone's heartbreak into a spectacle. I lowered my camera, ashamed of my intention. The scene before me unfolded in silence, yet it spoke volumes. Families, torn apart for years, meeting at the fence for mere minutes. Fathers holding their children's fingers through the cold metal bars, mothers wiping away tears they couldn't fully release. And all they could do was exchange a few words, share stories, and press their fingertips together—just that fleeting moment of human connection was enough to sustain them.

As I stood there, the weight of it all hit me. These people, living parallel lives on opposite sides of an unforgiving border, carried a pain that I could never truly understand. But I could feel it. In their eyes, in their trembling hands, in the unspoken love that passed between them. My heart ached. The air was thick with sadness and longing, but there was also an undeniable resilience—love still transcended those metal bars.

Ricardo told us about the many organizations fighting to reunite these families, like Al Otro Lado, providing legal help to migrants and refugees, and Border Angels, offering humanitarian aid. These groups are lifelines in a sea of despair, helping people navigate a system that seems designed to keep them apart.

As we left the fence behind, the sadness lingered in my heart. This wasn't the typical joy of travel that I was used to. It was a sobering reminder of how easily we take freedom and togetherness for granted. Despite the beautiful places I had seen, this was a moment of truth—a truth about borders, about separation, and about the human need for connection.

Later, we visited a local market. Ricardo proudly showed us the variety of fruits and vegetables sold there. He pointed out a spiky fruit that made me smile—jackfruit. As someone from Kerala, I was amused to see something so familiar in a foreign land. Jackfruit, tapioca, tamarind—foods that grew in my backyard were now part of this new experience, connecting me back to home even in the midst of this unfamiliar place.

At the market, we sampled a variety of local foods—everything from fresh fruit to delicious snacks. Then, we stumbled upon a stall that had an array of sauces. The shopkeeper proudly pointed to one bottle and said, "This one here is extremely spicy, so be careful!"

Now, this was my moment. A little voice inside me said, "This is your chance to show off your South Indian spice tolerance." With a grin, I confidently replied, "I'm from the South of India. We practically eat fire for breakfast! Spicy food is in my blood, so I'll give it a try."

I could see the others looking at me, probably wondering if I was some sort of spice-eating superhero. And well, my ego had already written the check, so I had to cash it. I grabbed a chip, dipped it generously in the sauce, and popped it into my mouth with a casual air, like I had done this a million times.

The moment the sauce hit my tongue, time slowed down. My brain, however, was screaming in fast-forward: "Abort mission! ABORT MISSION!" It felt like a volcano had erupted in my mouth, sending waves of fire to every corner of my being. My eyes started watering so fast, it was like someone had turned on the faucet. My face turned red, and my tongue was doing a panicked dance, desperately trying to escape the heat.

But pride is a funny thing. Despite my mouth being in full meltdown mode, I couldn't let anyone see the spicy sauce had absolutely destroyed me. So I did what any self-respecting spice warrior would do—I pretended everything was fine. I smiled (or at least tried to), gave a thumbs up, and said in the most strained voice ever, "Yeah, that's got a bit of a kick!"

In reality, my internal monologue was something like, "Water! Water! Somebody get me a fire extinguisher!" But there was no way I was going to ask for help. I just stood there, eyes watering, silently burning, while pretending to be completely unfazed. Ricardo and the others looked impressed, but little did they know I was barely holding it together. My pride stayed intact, but my taste buds had gone on strike.

I left that stall feeling victorious—kind of. Sure, I had survived the spiciest sauce I'd ever tasted, but I couldn't feel my tongue for the rest of the day. Moral of the story: Sometimes it's okay to admit when something is too spicy, even if you're from South India!

As I wandered through the vibrant local market, completely immersed in the sights, sounds, and especially the flavors, I felt as though I had stepped into another world. Each stall seemed to burst with life—vendors passionately offering their wares, the air thick with the smell of fresh tortillas, sizzling meat, and the sweet scent of tropical fruits. I was savoring every bite, every moment, lost in conversations with a few friendly locals who had welcomed me with open arms, eager to share stories and a taste of their rich culture.

In my blissful state, I hadn't noticed that I had positioned myself squarely in the middle of a narrow passage between two stalls. It wasn't a huge space to begin with, and my presence, unintentional as it was, created a bit of a traffic jam. People, bags in hand, were trying to weave their way through the bustling market, and there I was—oblivious, absorbed in sampling food and laughter.

It wasn't until I turned around that the realization hit me. I froze for a moment, taken aback. To my surprise, behind me stood a line of people, quietly waiting for me to move. I felt a wave of embarrassment wash over me, the kind that makes your face flush with heat. I had been so wrapped up in my own experience that I hadn't even noticed them standing there.

In that instant, I expected the worst. I braced myself for annoyed expressions, impatient sighs, or perhaps a sharp word or two about inconsiderate tourists. After all, I had caused an inconvenience, and in many places, that's more than enough to trigger some frustration. My mind raced, and I hurriedly blurted out a heartfelt apology, "Oh, I'm so sorry! I didn't realize I was in the way!"

But what happened next completely caught me off guard. Instead of irritation, what I saw were warm smiles—genuine, understanding smiles. One man chuckled lightly and waved his hand, as if to say, "It's nothing." An older woman, balancing bags of fresh produce, patted me on the arm and said softly, "No worries, amigo. It's okay, enjoy yourself." Another person simply smiled and nodded, as if the whole situation was more amusing than anything else.

There was no rush, no impatience, no pressure to move faster. They could see that I was a tourist, likely lost in the excitement of discovering their world, and rather than being frustrated by my thoughtlessness, they chose to embrace it with grace. These people, who had every right to be annoyed, instead offered me kindness. They waited patiently, without complaint, allowing me the space to enjoy the moment, even if it meant a brief delay in their day.

I was stunned. It was such a small gesture, but in its simplicity, it spoke volumes about the generosity and warmth of the Mexican people. Their patience wasn't just politeness—it was a reflection of their deeply ingrained culture of hospitality, their understanding that life isn't always about rushing from one place to another. They didn't see me as an inconvenience; they saw me as a fellow human, a guest in their country, and they welcomed me without hesitation.

It was a humbling experience, one that made me pause and reflect on how we often forget the value of patience and grace in our fast-paced lives. The kindness I was shown that day in the market was something rare and precious, a reminder that hospitality isn't just about opening your home to someone—it's about opening your heart, too.

As I moved aside to let them pass, I couldn't help but feel a deep sense of gratitude. These people, who could have easily brushed me off or hurried me along, instead left me with a memory that I will cherish forever. Their smiles, their warmth, their quiet understanding—it was a testament to the beauty of the human spirit and the capacity for kindness in the most ordinary of moments.

In that market, on that day, I learned something far more valuable than anything I had anticipated. I came expecting to see a new country, to taste new food, to experience new sights. But what I left with was a renewed faith in humanity, and a deep respect for a people who showed me that, sometimes, the greatest joy comes not from what we do, but how we treat others.

If anyone were to ask me now what I think of Mexico and its people, I would tell them this: they are some of the best people I have ever met. The Mexicans taught me an important lesson—don't let preconceived notions and headlines define your perception of a place or its people. Go, experience it for yourself, and you just might discover something beautiful, as I did.

CHAPTER III

Istanbul – My Experiences with the Natives

Some cities have a way of calling to you, even before you ever set foot on their streets. For me, Istanbul was one of those places. I'd read countless articles about its stunning architecture, heard friends rave about the food, and watched travel shows that showcased the city's vibrant, layered life. It wasn't just another destination on my list—it felt like a place I *needed* to experience. So when the opportunity presented itself in 2019, I knew I had to seize it.

I was on my way back from a conference in San Diego, USA, and browsing Turkish Airlines' website when I saw their stopover program. Three days in Istanbul. It sounded perfect. Just enough time to dip my toes into this magical city without stretching my budget. The best part? My travel grant covered most of the expenses, so I couldn't resist.

As the plane began its descent over the Bosphorus, a flutter of excitement built up inside me. The sprawling city lay below—ancient minarets mingling with modern skyscrapers, all glistening under the golden autumn sun. It was a sight that instantly captivated me. Even from the air, I knew this would be no ordinary layover.

Istanbul greeted me with crisp autumn air, the scent of roasted chestnuts wafting from street vendors, and the distant hum of a bustling metropolis. With only three days to explore, I was determined to make every moment count.

I booked a hotel near Taksim Square, the heart of European Istanbul. It was close to major attractions like the Blue Mosque, Hagia Sophia, and of course, the lively Taksim Square itself. As I unpacked, the excitement bubbled up again. But something told me that if I tried navigating this ancient city on my own, I'd miss out on its hidden gems. So, I turned to Airbnb for help.

As I scrolled through their experiences, one listing jumped out at me: a four-hour guided video tour of Istanbul hosted by Hazel, a student at a University in Istanbul. What intrigued me wasn't just the promise of exploring Istanbul's history and food but the fact that they would film the whole experience and send me a video afterward. For someone who was toying with the idea of starting a YouTube channel, it seemed like the perfect way to dip my toes into the world of travel vlogging.

The next morning, I stood in Taksim Square, the cool autumn breeze brushing against my face. The square was quiet, with the city just waking up. I was nervous but excited—this was my first time traveling alone in a city so full of life and history. Just then, I spotted Hazel and her friend Usman walking toward me. They both had an easygoing energy that immediately put me at ease.

"Are you ready for the best four hours of your life?" Hazel asked, her eyes twinkling with excitement.

"I hope so," I replied, smiling, trying to hide the fact that I had no idea what to expect.

We started by exploring the narrow streets near Istiklal Avenue. Hazel and Usman were students, using their love for Istanbul to earn a little extra cash by guiding tourists around the city. Their passion for the city was contagious. As we strolled, they shared anecdotes about the places we passed. Every street seemed to have a story, every corner a bit of history I wouldn't have known without them.

Our first stop was a cozy café where I had my first taste of a traditional Turkish breakfast. The spread was overwhelming—freshly baked bread, a variety of cheeses, olives, jams, and honey. But the star of the meal was a drink I'd never encountered before—*pickled juice*. Hazel poured me a glass with a grin.

"You'll love this. It's spicy, tangy... refreshing. And trust me, it'll wake you up," she said.

As someone who grew up in South India, where spice is an essential part of life, I was intrigued. I took a sip, and the fiery, tangy flavor hit me like a burst of energy. "This is amazing!" I exclaimed, already planning a second glass.

"Told you!" Hazel laughed. "It's like a secret weapon here."

Later, we wandered through bustling markets, where the smell of freshly brewed Turkish coffee filled the air. Usman, noticing my curiosity, led me to a street vendor selling *midye*—stuffed mussels with lemon. He handed me one, squeezing a bit of lemon onto the shell.

"Try it. It's a must," Usman said with a wink.

I took a bite, savoring the briny, rich flavor of the mussels. It was a simple, but delicious snack, and I felt a sense of accomplishment as I captured the moment on my phone for

Instagram. But my excitement was short-lived. Moments later, my friend Mustafa, an Istanbul native, commented on the post: "Be careful. Mussels here are often collected from contaminated waters."

My stomach sank. "Did I just eat something unsafe?" I asked Hazel, suddenly feeling uneasy.

She shrugged, "It's hit or miss. But don't worry too much. You'll be fine!"

The thrill of trying something new turned into a brief moment of regret, but I decided to shake it off. After all, travel is full of unexpected moments, and sometimes, you just have to roll with them.

The tour continued with Hazel and Usman taking me through some lesser-known spots, and by the end of the day, I had a new appreciation for Istanbul—and myself. When I received the video of the tour a week later, I watched myself walking through the city, laughing, exploring, and tasting new things. That video sparked something inside me, something I had been hesitant to act on. I realized I had a story to tell, and Istanbul was the perfect place to start.

My second day was no less eventful. After visiting some local landmarks, I decided to exchange money at a center near

Taksim Square. Having relied on the airport ATM earlier, I hadn't realized how much better the rates would be at the local exchange centers. As I walked away with a handful of Turkish lira, I couldn't help but feel like I had won a small victory. It was one of those mundane travel tasks that felt oddly triumphant, a little moment of success in a foreign land.

That night, I reflected on my brief time in Istanbul. What had begun as a casual stopover had turned into a journey of self-discovery. Not only had I fallen in love with the city's vibrant culture, but I had found the confidence to start my YouTube channel, *Mirabile*.

One of the first things that struck me when I landed in Istanbul was how affordable everything seemed compared to the city I call home. Whether it was food, clothing, or souvenirs, nothing felt like it would break the bank. In fact, I was amazed by how far my money could stretch. After exploring a bit on my first day, I ventured into the local markets and shops, picking up some dresses, curios, and souvenirs for my family. The quality of the goods was top-notch, and the prices were a dream—so much so that I found myself tempted to buy more than I had initially planned!

While browsing Airbnb for another tour, I stumbled upon an experience titled, "View Cheapest Local Bazaars and Save

40% Cost." Now, who could resist an offer like that? I certainly couldn't! That's how I was introduced to Mr. Ramnath, a PhD scholar from Bangladesh. When I first met him, he greeted me with a warm smile and said, "Brother, you're going to love this tour. Trust me, these local markets have some of the best deals, but you have to know how to bargain."

He guided me to a metro station and from there, the real adventure began. Ramnath was not only knowledgeable about the local markets, but he was a master at haggling. Watching him negotiate with the shopkeepers was a thing of beauty—he would smile, crack a joke in Turkish, and magically, the price would drop! Thanks to him, I managed to buy items at a much lower price than what I'd paid the previous day.

At one point, I was eyeing a beautifully embroidered jacket. Ramnath noticed my hesitation and whispered, "Just wait." He strolled over to the shopkeeper and began chatting. After a few minutes of back-and-forth, Ramnath gave me a nod. The price had dropped by 30%! I couldn't believe it. I turned to him and said, "You've got to teach me how you do that!"

He laughed and replied, "It's all in the charm, my friend. Never rush, and always act like you're ready to walk away."

The experience with Ramnath was incredible, and I left the markets that day feeling like I had truly discovered the heart of Istanbul's shopping scene.

On my second day, I decided to book another tour—this time through an app called *Showaround*. A local guide named Sali arrived at my hotel that afternoon. She was a striking woman, with a warm smile and a no-nonsense attitude that immediately set the tone for our tour.

"Are you ready to walk?" she asked with a mischievous grin.

I, full of excitement and optimism, replied, "Absolutely, let's go!"

Big mistake.

Sali was an energetic whirlwind, and the moment we set off, I realized I had seriously underestimated her pace. She moved through the streets of Istanbul like someone on a mission, while I trailed behind, trying to catch my breath. At one point, I jokingly called out, "Are you training for a marathon or something?"

She turned back, laughing, "You've got to keep up! We've got a lot to see."

We visited several historical landmarks—places steeped in history that I wouldn't have found on my own. As we wandered through the old markets, Sali shared fascinating insights about the city's past, its Ottoman heritage, and the daily lives of the locals. Listening to her stories, I felt like I was stepping back in time. It wasn't just a tour; it was an immersion into Istanbul's rich tapestry of culture and history.

While walking through the Grand Bazaar, Sali noticed I was eyeing a beautiful traditional Turkish teacup set. "Perfect for a gift," she said, nudging me.

"I was thinking the same for my wife," I responded.

"You should definitely get it. And don't forget, bargain!" she added with a wink.

Thanks to her advice, I ended up with not just the teacup set but a few other random souvenirs. The shopkeepers were friendly and the atmosphere vibrant—it was one of those moments that made me fall even more in love with the city.

As evening approached, Sali suggested we grab dinner at a local restaurant. "You must try *raki*," she said with a playful grin. "It's a strong Turkish alcohol. Tradition says you have to drink it with friends."

Intrigued, I agreed. We toasted with small glasses of the anise-flavored spirit, and the warm buzz of the raki mixed with the soft glow of the Istanbul evening. It was different from anything I'd tasted before, but it had a boldness that I appreciated. After my first glass, I ordered a second.

But Sali quickly leaned over, her expression serious this time. "Careful now. *Raki* is strong. Too much, and you'll regret it tomorrow."

Heeding her advice, I switched to a Turkish beer instead, savoring the rest of the meal with a lighter buzz and enjoying our conversation. We laughed, shared stories, and by the end of the night, I felt like I had made a true connection with the city—not just as a tourist, but as someone who had experienced it with locals.

As my short trip to Istanbul came to an end, I found myself already longing to return. The sights, the people, the food—it had all left an indelible mark on me. When I think back on that whirlwind adventure, I can't help but smile at the memories, and the sense of excitement I felt in every corner of the city.

"I'll be back," I thought to myself as I boarded my flight. And even now, I'm eagerly looking forward to the day when I can return to that magical place.

CHAPTER IV

Have You Ever Missed a Flight

The Airline staff checked the status and regretfully informed us that we are late and can't travel in that flight. It was such a shock for us that I can't express it in words now...........

On May 2019, my family and I embarked on what was meant to be a dream trip to Italy. It had been meticulously planned—a journey through Italy, Austria, and Switzerland, culminating with a return flight from Milan to Riyadh, via London. We had booked our tickets through British Airways, and everything was running smoothly until our return on June 5th.

We were scheduled to land at London Heathrow at 12:45 p.m., with just one hour to make our connecting flight to Riyadh. A tight connection, sure, but manageable—or so we thought. What we didn't account for was that, on that very same day, U.S. President Donald Trump was wrapping up his state visit to the UK. As a result, air traffic around Heathrow was backed up, causing delays across multiple flights, including ours. Our plane landed in London over an hour late, and the sense of urgency hit the moment we touched down.

"We have to move fast!" I said to my wife as the plane taxied to the gate. My son, equally concerned, echoed my thoughts, "I hope we make it, Dad."

As soon as the seatbelt sign turned off, we bolted towards the transit gate, boarding passes clutched tightly in hand. Our hearts were racing as we reached the automated gates, only to be greeted by an error message on the screen. The gate wouldn't open. Confused, we stood there for a moment before an airport staff member directed us to the British Airways counter nearby.

"Let's go!" I urged my family, and we hurried to the counter, hoping against hope that we could still make it.

The British Airways staff, a composed woman in her late 30s, scanned our tickets and after a brief pause, she looked up with an expression of regret. "I'm sorry," she said gently, "but you've missed the flight. There's nothing we can do now."

Her words hit me like a brick. "What do you mean?" I stammered. "We just landed late, there must be some way we can get on board."

"I understand," she replied calmly, "but the gates are closed, and the plane is about to take off. Unfortunately, you'll have to be rebooked on another flight."

I stood there, unable to process the situation. My wife, seeing the look of shock on my face, gently squeezed my hand, whispering, "It's going to be fine, we'll figure it out."

"Okay, so what are our options?" I finally asked, forcing myself to stay calm.

The woman began typing furiously into her computer. "There's a flight to Jeddah later this evening," she offered.

I quickly shook my head, "No, Jeddah is too far from Riyadh. Is there anything else?"

After a few more minutes of searching, she looked up and said, "We can book you on the next British Airways flight to Riyadh, but it's not until tomorrow."

I could hardly contain my excitement. An unexpected stopover in London, a city we hadn't visited in years, and all without having to pay for it! But I didn't want to appear too eager, so I nodded stoically. "Alright," I said, "book us on that flight."

As she arranged the bookings, I glanced at my wife, whose face was lit up with barely contained joy. I knew what she was thinking—an extra day in London was a blessing in disguise. Trying to play it cool, I whispered, "You might want to sit down before you give it away!"

Once the rebooking was complete, the British Airways staff handed us hotel vouchers, shuttle tickets, and meal coupons. "Your accommodation and meals are all covered," she said. "Enjoy your stay in London."

I walked away from the counter, my heart soaring with the thought of an unexpected day in London. "Well, looks like we've got ourselves a bonus vacation!" I said, grinning at my wife and son.

Our excitement was short-lived as we approached the immigration counter. The officer, a stern-looking man in a crisp uniform, glanced at our passports. His expression remained unmoved as he handed them back. "Sorry, you don't have a UK visa," he said, his voice flat, as if delivering routine bad news. "You won't be able to enter the country."

I felt my heart drop into my stomach. This couldn't be happening. Not after we'd already gone through so much. "But we're only here for a day," I began, my voice tinged with desperation. "We have U.S. visas. Could you check if we could use those?"

The officer paused for a moment, then gave us a thoughtful look. His demeanor softened slightly. "I'm not sure," he admitted, "but let me check with my supervisor." He motioned for us to follow him, and we trailed behind, nerves fraying with each step. The possibility of spending 24 hours stuck in the sterile confines of the airport weighed heavily on us. We reached a small, nondescript office and were told to sit down.

My wife glanced at me, her eyes wide with concern. I tried to offer her a reassuring smile, but inside, I was as anxious as she was. Time seemed to stretch endlessly as we sat in silence, the minutes crawling by, the uncertainty hanging in the air like a thick fog. "What now?" I thought. Were we going to be trapped here, just steps away from a whole city we had explored in the past, but now could only gaze at longingly?

It felt like hours, though it was probably only fifteen minutes, when the officer finally returned. His face had changed—there was something resembling a smile. "Good news!" he said, much to our relief. "Since you have U.S. visas, we can issue you a 24-hour transit visa. You're free to enjoy your day in the UK."

As he handed us back our passports, a sense of relief washed over me—but I couldn't help but feel a sharp pang of irony. "Well, that's a first," I muttered to my wife as we walked away. "I've been to the UK several times, and this is the first time I've met a nice immigration officer."

She raised an eyebrow. "Really?"

"Every other time," I continued, my tone dropping into disbelief, "they acted like we'd come to steal something." I recalled the stiff interrogations, the way they'd scrutinize my documents, as though I had some hidden agenda. "It's ridiculous," I added, shaking my head. "They behave like we're the ones trying to rob them—when, in reality, they've already stolen everything from us."

My wife shot me a knowing look. "Including the Kohinoor diamond," she said, a smirk playing on her lips.

"Exactly," I whispered, glancing back over my shoulder to make sure no one had overheard. The irony of it all made me chuckle, though it was laced with the bitterness of our shared history. "The British took all they could from India, including the Kohinoor, but still act like we're the ones with sticky fingers."

My son, who had been quietly following along, suddenly piped up. "What's the Kohinoor?"

I glanced at him, momentarily surprised by the question, and then sighed. "It's a diamond, buddy," I explained briefly. "A really big, really famous one that used to be in India before the British took it." I wasn't sure if this was the time to dive into the murky waters of colonialism, but I could see the gears turning in his mind.

"And now it's in a crown," my wife chimed in, winking at him. "But today, we're not thinking about that. Today, we're taking back something much better—a free day in London!"

Her playful tone snapped us all out of the seriousness, and we laughed. I couldn't help but feel a little triumphant, though. Here we were, three generations of Indians, walking freely in the streets of London with nothing but a 24-hour transit visa. It might have been a small victory, but it felt like a symbolic one.

We grabbed a quick lunch at the airport and then hopped on the shuttle to our hotel. After freshening up, we headed straight out to explore London. Our first stop was the London Eye, where we marveled at the city's iconic skyline, followed by some impromptu shopping and visits to a few of the city's famous landmarks.

"Isn't this amazing?" my wife said as we strolled through the streets of London. "This feels like a second vacation."

"Absolutely," I agreed, grinning. "And it's all on British Airways!"

By the time we returned to the hotel at 9 p.m., exhausted but happy, we felt as though we had truly made the most of our unexpected layover.

The next day, after a hearty breakfast, we made our way back to Heathrow, boarded our flight, and returned to Riyadh without a hitch.

A week after we got back, something interesting caught my eye. While scrolling through Facebook, I came across a post in a travel group about *AirHelp*, a website that helps travelers claim compensation for delayed or canceled flights. I paused. Should I try this? After all, British Airways had treated us well—free accommodation, meals, and a chance to spend a day in London. Would it be right to claim compensation too?

I voiced my doubts to a friend, who was quick to reply. "It's your right. The law says if your flight is delayed, you're entitled to compensation. You should go for it."

That convinced me. I logged onto AirHelp's website and submitted my documents, including our boarding passes, tickets, and passports. A few months passed, during which AirHelp kept me updated on the progress of my claim.

Then came the news I had been waiting for. I received an email from AirHelp stating that I was eligible for compensation—€1,800! However, AirHelp would take a commission of €900. Even so, I would still walk away with €900—about $1,000. Considering that our entire flight to

Milan had cost $1,535 for the three of us, I was essentially getting half of our vacation refunded.

As I shared the news with friends, some joked, "Next time, we'll book flights with tight layovers and hope for a delay!"

But I reminded them, "It was a lucky break for us this time, but if it had been an urgent situation—like an important meeting—it could've been a disaster. Plan wisely!"

In the end, what had begun as a nerve-wracking situation turned into a free London vacation and a partial refund of our entire trip. Talk about a silver lining!

CHAPTER V

Lake Como, Italy

In the spring of 2019, my good friend Mr. Muath proposed an enticing plan for our Ramadan holiday—an 11-day journey through the charming villages of Europe. The idea of a scenic escape, traveling through breathtaking landscapes and historical towns, was irresistible. With my wife and son by my side, we eagerly embraced the adventure ahead, unaware of the surprises and memories that awaited us.

We began our journey with a British Airways flight from Riyadh to Milan, with a short layover in London. The anticipation buzzed around us as we touched down in Milan, our spirits high. The first task on arrival: getting a local SIM card for communication. A quick stop at the airport sorted that, and we were on to the car rental agency, where our pre-booked vehicle awaited. Our itinerary was ambitious—Italy, Austria, and Switzerland. But little did we know, a twist was just around the corner.

As we approached the counter, the rental agent greeted us warmly. After some pleasantries, the agent informed us, with a regretful look on his face, "I'm sorry, sir, but you won't be able to take this car into Austria."

I frowned, taken aback. "But we specifically chose this rental because it covers multiple countries."

He shrugged sympathetically. "Unfortunately, due to the car insurance policy, it's not allowed for this vehicle."

A brief silence followed as we exchanged worried glances. My son looked up at me expectantly. My wife sighed. "What do we do now?" she asked.

I took a breath and smiled. "No problem! We'll adjust the plan. Italy and Switzerland alone will be more than enough."

With that, our adventure began.

Our first destination was Schignano, a hidden gem nestled along the serene shores of Lake Como in Italy's Lombardy region. As we drove through the meandering roads, flanked by towering Alps, I couldn't help but reminisce about the winding hill roads of Kerala, my homeland. "It's just like driving through the Western Ghats," I said, my voice filled with nostalgia as we navigated the tunnels through the Alpine peaks.

My wife smiled. "But with a lot more snow," she added, pointing at the white-tipped mountains.

After a picturesque drive, we arrived in Schignano. It was even more beautiful than I had imagined—quaint, quiet, and surrounded by Italy's untouched natural beauty. The air felt fresher here, the kind of place where time slows down, and the world outside fades into the distance.

We had chosen an Airbnb homestay for our stay, hosted by a kind man named Mr. Antonio and his wife. As they welcomed us into their charming residence, we felt immediately at ease. The house, a cozy two-bedroom with a lovely living area and a kitchen, had a balcony bursting with colorful flowers. "It's perfect," my wife whispered, taking in the view.

Antonio smiled warmly, handing us the keys. "We've stocked the kitchen for you," he said in broken English. "Eggs, bread, milk—just in case. It's Sunday tomorrow, and most shops will be closed."

I felt a wave of gratitude. "That's very thoughtful of you," I replied. "Thank you so much." Their gesture was a reminder of how generous and kind people could be, and it added a special warmth to the start of our journey.

That evening, after a quiet stroll through the empty streets of Schignano—lined with century-old buildings and homestays—we returned to the villa, our hearts content and our minds eager for the days ahead.

The next morning, we set off for the famous Lake Como. Our plan was simple—explore the city, enjoy the scenic drives, and indulge in some local cuisine. As we drove through the winding roads, my son gazed out the window. "Is that Lake Como?" he asked, his eyes wide with wonder.

I nodded. "That's right. It's the third-largest lake in Italy and one of the deepest, over 400 meters!"

My wife chimed in, "They say it's shaped like the letter Y because it was formed by glaciers."

Our first stop along the lake was the town of Argegno, a small, charming village on the water's edge. We wandered through the cobblestone streets, marveling at the old buildings and the breathtaking sight of yachts swaying gently in the harbor. A small church stood proudly in the town center, its façade weathered by time, yet beautiful in its simplicity. "Look at this view," my wife said, snapping a picture. "It's like something out of a postcard."

Soon, we realized we needed to park. But there was one small hiccup: the parking meters only accepted coins, and we had none. Just as frustration began to set in, a friendly

Israeli couple noticed our struggle. "Do you need help with the parking?" the man asked.

I smiled sheepishly. "Yes, thank you. We didn't realize it was coin-only."

With a laugh, they offered us some change, helping us navigate the local parking system. It was another reminder that kindness transcends borders.

Feeling adventurous, we decided to take a boat tour around Lake Como, as suggested by our new friends. At the ferry counter, I asked the attendant, "What's a good option for a half-day tour?"

She thought for a moment before replying, "Take the ferry to Lenno. It's a beautiful town, and the ride is peaceful."

Without hesitation, we bought tickets and boarded the two-story ferry. Settling into our window seats, we watched as the boat glided across the lake, the Alps rising majestically in the distance. The water shimmered under the soft afternoon sun, and the sight of wild geese floating along only added to the charm. "This is incredible," my son murmured, his eyes glued to the view.

Lenno was a quiet town, much less crowded than the others around the lake. "It's exactly what we wanted," my wife said as we strolled along the peaceful streets, taking in the sights. We stumbled upon Villa del Balbianello, a stunning villa perched on the hillside, famous for its appearance in Star Wars: Episode II. Unfortunately, a wedding was in full swing, and the villa was closed to visitors. "Just our luck," I said with a chuckle. "We'll have to admire it from here."

We continued exploring, visiting the Church of Saint Stefano and the Baptistery of St. John. "These buildings are so old," my son said, his voice filled with awe. "I can't believe they're still standing."

"Centuries of history," I added, running my hand along the weathered stone. "There's so much to learn here."

Before leaving Lenno, we wandered into a small souvenir shop run by a cheerful elderly woman. Her English was limited, but her smile was warm as she showed us around. We picked out fridge magnets and keychains—small tokens to remind us of this special place.

Our last stop before heading back to Schignano was Argegno, where the charm of the lakeside scenery drew us back for one final culinary adventure. The sun hung low in the sky, casting a warm golden hue over the tranquil waters of Lake Como as we approached a quaint restaurant nestled along the shore. The scent of garlic and fresh herbs wafted through the air, making our mouths water in anticipation.

Upon entering, we were greeted by a cheerful hostess who ushered us to a cozy table overlooking the lake. The ambiance was rustic, with wooden beams and soft lighting that created an inviting atmosphere. As we settled in, I noticed the menu was entirely in Italian, a delightful challenge for our little family.

"Well, this will be fun," I said, scanning the options. "Looks like we're in for an adventure."

My wife chuckled, glancing over my shoulder. "At least we can point and pray for the best!"

The waitress, a young woman with a warm smile, approached our table. She introduced herself but quickly realized our language barrier. "Parla Italiano?" she asked, her voice friendly yet hopeful.

"Um, just a little," I replied, feeling a mix of excitement and trepidation.

"No English?" she inquired, her eyes sparkling with encouragement.

I nodded, and we all shared a laugh. "I guess we'll have to do this the old-fashioned way," I joked, pointing at the pictures on the menu.

We made our selections, relying on the vivid images to guide us. My wife pointed to a dish that looked like a seafood pasta, while I opted for a classic spaghetti pomodoro.

As we waited, we chatted about our day, our eyes wandering to the picturesque view outside. The lake shimmered in the fading light, boats bobbing gently in the water. "Can you believe we're here?" my wife asked, her voice tinged with awe. "This feels like a dream."

Moments later, our dishes arrived, and they were a feast for the senses. The pasta glistened with a rich sauce, and the seafood was beautifully arranged atop a bed of perfectly cooked noodles.

"This is what I call authentic," my wife said, a satisfied smile spreading across her face as she savored a forkful of her dish. "I can't believe we're eating this right by the lake."

With our hearts and bellies full, we left the restaurant, stepping back into the gentle evening air, ready to soak in the last moments of our enchanting day in Italy.

As the sun set over the lake, casting a golden glow across the water, I felt a deep sense of contentment. Our journey had only just begun, but already it was full of unforgettable moments—unexpected detours, new friendships, and a glimpse into the soul of Europe's beautiful villages. "Next stop, Switzerland," I said with a grin, knowing that more adventures awaited us just across the border.

CHAPTER VI

From Touchdowns to Tastebuds: Tales of Triumphs and Tastings in New Orleans!

New Orleans, famously known as the birthplace of jazz and a melting pot of cultures, beckons travelers with its vibrant atmosphere, rich history, and delectable cuisine. As I embarked on my journey from the bustling streets of New York to the enchanting bayous of Louisiana, I couldn't shake the feeling that my visit to the Crescent City would be an unforgettable adventure.

Upon landing at Louis Armstrong New Orleans International Airport, the warm Southern hospitality enveloped me like a comforting blanket. I hopped into an

Uber for the ride to my apartment, and my driver, David, turned out to be a treasure trove of local knowledge.

"Welcome to the Big Easy!" he exclaimed, glancing at me in the rearview mirror. "You're in for a real treat."

"I can't wait! Any must-dos while I'm here?" I asked, eager for tips.

"Oh, I've got a list!" He chuckled, pulling out his phone. "Let me airdrop you my insider's guide. You'll want to experience the food, the music, and definitely catch a football game."

With his recommendations in hand, I felt like I had a map to hidden treasures just waiting to be uncovered.

The next day, we followed David's suggestion to attend a live football match at the Caesars Superdome, a rite of passage for any visitor. As we approached the stadium, the air buzzed with excitement, fans clad in gold and black shouting chants, and vendors hawking team merchandise.

"This is incredible!" my friend said, his eyes wide with wonder. "I've never seen anything like it!"

But as we neared the ticket booth, reality hit hard.

"Sold out?" I echoed, staring at the sign in disbelief. "But we were so looking forward to this!"

The disappointment was palpable as we learned the available tickets were either gone or far beyond our budget.

"What do we do now?" my friend asked, glancing around at the swirling mass of fans.

"Let's not let this ruin our day. There's still so much energy out here!" I replied, trying to keep our spirits high.

Instead of sulking, we decided to embrace the vibrant pre-game festivities. We wandered the area, soaking in the atmosphere, the pulsating beats of music filling the air, and the tantalizing aromas wafting from nearby food stalls.

"Look at everyone having a good time," I said, nodding toward a group of fans dancing in the street.

"You're right! Let's join in!" my friend laughed, pulling me toward the revelry.

Despite not being inside the stadium, we cheered with fellow fans, high-fived strangers, and snapped pictures, united in our shared love for the game.

"This is a testament to the charm of New Orleans," I mused, soaking it all in. "Sometimes the best memories happen unexpectedly."

While I reflected on our ticket mishap, I felt a twinge of regret for not planning ahead. However, this experience reminded me that spontaneity often leads to the most memorable adventures. I vowed to check and book tickets in advance next time, but I couldn't help but smile at the joy we found right outside the Superdome.

Later that evening, our adventure continued as we stumbled upon Harrah's New Orleans casino. The allure of the lively atmosphere beckoned us inside.

"I've never gambled before," I admitted to my friend as we stepped into the dazzling world of lights and sounds.

"Neither have I, but why not give it a shot? It could be fun!" he replied, excitement dancing in his eyes.

With $150 set aside for gaming, I felt a rush of curiosity as I approached a blackjack table. Despite a few wins, luck soon turned against me, and I watched my budget dwindle.

"Don't worry about it," my friend said, trying to comfort me. "We're here to have fun, right?"

He was right. The camaraderie among fellow gamers, the anticipation in the air, and even the complimentary drinks made the evening enjoyable.

"This place is wild!" I shouted over the noise, laughter bubbling up as I reveled in the thrill of it all.

Reflecting on my time at Harrah's, I realized that gambling could be exhilarating, but moderation was key. Setting a budget helped me enjoy the experience without overindulging.

As I left the casino, a smile plastered on my face, I appreciated the unexpected adventure that unfolded in the heart of New Orleans.

Fuelled by David's enthusiastic recommendations, we dove into the culinary scene of New Orleans with great anticipation. The thought of tasting authentic local dishes thrilled us, so we wasted no time in ordering a Po'boy with shrimp at a nearby eatery.

"This is supposed to be amazing," I said, my mouth watering in anticipation.

But when the dish arrived, disappointment settled in. The fried shrimp nestled in the bread was lackluster, lacking the bold flavors we had imagined.

"Hmm, this isn't what I expected," I confessed, glancing at my friend, who nodded in agreement. "Maybe David's tastes are different from ours."

Undeterred, we pressed on to explore another beloved New Orleans delicacy: oysters.

"These better be good," my friend joked as we sat down to sample the briny treat.

As we savored the oysters, their freshness danced on our tongues, and we both sighed in delight.

"Now, this is what I call redemption," I said, beaming as I squeezed lemon over another oyster.

Feeling adventurous, we decided to try a renowned restaurant for steak the following evening. The ambiance was inviting, and the cocktails were exquisite, but our excitement dimmed when the steak arrived, failing to impress us.

"What a letdown," I murmured, shaking my head.

Disheartened, we made a pact to retreat to the comfort of our accommodation for the remainder of our stay, opting to prepare our own meals.

"Sometimes the best meals are the ones made at home," my friend said, smiling as we gathered ingredients.

Bidding farewell to the bustling streets of New Orleans, we carried with us a newfound appreciation for culinary exploration and the importance of embracing the unexpected.

Our taste buds may not have been fully satisfied, but our hearts were full of memories from a city steeped in culture and history.

Our adventures led us to the Sazerac House for a complimentary tour, where we delved into the rich legacy of our favorite drinks.

"I've always wanted to learn about the Sazerac cocktail!" I exclaimed as we entered the stunning venue.

The engaging exhibits brought the history of the Sazerac to life, showcasing its integral role in the customs and culture of New Orleans.

"Did you know it originated in the 1850s?" I asked my friend, who listened intently.

The tour allowed us to appreciate the craftsmanship behind every sip, where tradition met innovation.

"Every drink tells a story," I remarked, savoring a complimentary sample. "This is more than just a cocktail; it's part of the city's heritage."

The Sazerac House was a celebration of the timeless allure of New Orleans' cocktail culture, leaving an indelible impression on us.

Eager to explore more of the cocktail scene, we ventured from one iconic bar to another, sampling the city's renowned libations.

"We have to try the Hand Grenade!" my friend insisted, recalling David's enthusiastic recommendation.

However, much to my disappointment, the drink didn't live up to its hype.

"Is it just me, or is this underwhelming?" I said, shaking my head as I took a sip.

"Definitely not my favorite either," my friend agreed.

Undeterred, we continued our cocktail journey, hopping between bars that each offered something unique. The diversity and creativity of the city's drinking culture fascinated me.

"Even if the Hand Grenade didn't impress, this has been such a fun night," I reflected as we toasted with our latest drinks.

David's curated list of recommendations opened up a world of unique adventures. From swamp tours to haunted history explorations, each suggestion promised to reveal the essence of New Orleans.

"I'm glad we didn't just stick to the tourist traps," I said, smiling as we wandered through the lively streets of the French Quarter.

Visiting the World War II Museum was particularly memorable, igniting a newfound interest in history that would stay with me long after my trip.

While the Cemetery tour and Ghost Hunt beckoned, I chose to follow my own interests, tailoring my experience to connect with the city in unexpected ways.

"You know, it's great to explore on our own terms," I remarked to my friend as we strolled down a picturesque street.

Reflecting on my time in New Orleans, I felt gratitude for the myriad experiences created. Beyond its surface allure, the city revealed a dynamic blend of culture, history, and hospitality that resonates with all who visit.

"There's something magical about this place," I said, looking out over the bustling streets.

I had high hopes for a city renowned for its vibrant culture, lively music scene, and acclaimed cuisine. However, I found that my experience didn't quite align with my expectations.

While the atmosphere was undeniably lively and the streets buzzed with energy, the food left me wanting more.

Many dishes I tried simply didn't resonate with my palate, and I was left feeling somewhat disappointed. The much-anticipated Po'boy and the famous gumbo didn't deliver the burst of flavors I had hoped for. It was a bit disheartening, especially given the city's reputation for culinary excellence.

That said, I fully acknowledge that this reflects my personal taste and preferences. New Orleans is a city with a rich culinary landscape, and what didn't work for me might be a delightful experience for someone else. The beauty of travel is that it exposes us to different flavors and styles, and while I didn't connect with the local cuisine, many visitors rave about it.

Ultimately, my experience serves as a reminder that every traveler's journey is unique. The magic of New Orleans is still evident in its music, culture, and history. While the food may not have been to my liking, it doesn't mean the city is any less captivating. It's all about individual choices and taste buds, and I encourage others to explore New Orleans with an open mind. You may discover your own hidden gems that resonate perfectly with your preferences!

CHAPTER VII

USS Intrepid: A Thrilling Journey Through History

In 2023, during my much-anticipated trip to New York, I stumbled upon the USS Intrepid Museum, and I couldn't contain my excitement. As a fan of war museums and monuments, the prospect of exploring this legendary aircraft carrier was thrilling. My research had quickly elevated the USS Intrepid Museum to the top of my must-visit list.

I was staying in the bustling heart of Times Square, surrounded by the dazzling lights and sounds of the city. When I realized the museum was just a 25-minute walk away, I decided to take the opportunity to stretch my legs and enjoy the fresh air. The morning was perfect, the temperature a comfortable 22 degrees. I thought to myself, "This is a great way to maintain my fitness routine while soaking in the city."

As I made my way through the vibrant streets, the hustle and bustle of New York surrounded me. Suddenly, disaster struck. My iPhone slipped from my hand and hit the pavement with a heart-stopping crack. Panic surged through me as I picked it up, dreading the worst. "Please be okay," I muttered under my breath. To my dismay, the back camera was shattered. My heart sank. Here I was, on a dream trip with over seven days left, and my phone was my primary tool for capturing memories. Buying a new one was out of the question given my budget constraints.

Just as I was about to spiral into despair, I took a closer look and discovered that the front camera was still functional. "Thank goodness for small mercies," I thought, relieved. I realized I could still take photos and videos, albeit with some limitations. With a renewed sense of determination, I continued my walk, refusing to let this mishap ruin my day.

As I approached the USS Intrepid, the sight of the massive ship against the skyline took my breath away. "Wow, look at that!" I exclaimed, my spirits lifting. This wasn't just a museum; it was a floating testament to history, a time capsule of bravery and innovation.

Stepping aboard the USS Intrepid felt like stepping back in time. The deck was lined with an impressive array of aircraft, each with its own story to tell. Fighter jets, helicopters, and reconnaissance planes—all meticulously restored—stood like silent sentinels of the past. I was particularly drawn to the sleek, menacing form of the Blackbird spy plane. "What secrets did you carry?" I wondered, captivated by its dark silhouette.

Inside the aircraft carrier, the atmosphere was electric. I noticed several veterans, who had served on the Intrepid, mingling with visitors, sharing their stories with a palpable sense of pride and nostalgia.

As I stepped onto the deck where the video was displayed, I was immediately enveloped by the deafening roar of engines and the thundering boom of anti-aircraft guns, creating a visceral experience that transported me to that tumultuous time. I was captivated by the sights and sounds, my heart racing as the scenes unfolded around me. Suddenly, a chilling video began to play, detailing a kamikaze attack on the USS Intrepid. The screen flickered to life with historical footage, showing the chaos and destruction that ensued as enemy aircraft dove toward the carrier. The narrator's voice echoed in the background, recounting the harrowing details. "If you were standing in the exact spot you are right now on that day," he said gravely, "you would have been dead in the attack."

A collective gasp rose from the crowd, a palpable sense of fear and awe settling over us. I turned to a fellow visitor, our eyes wide with disbelief. "Can you imagine?" I whispered, trying to grasp the magnitude of what had happened. The man nodded, his expression somber yet captivated.

The exhibit painted a vivid picture of the chaos and heroism of that day, making us feel the gravity of the moment. As the video continued, I felt an intense connection to the servicemen who had fought bravely, risking their lives in the face of such overwhelming danger. The immersive experience truly brought history to life, making the sacrifices of those who served feel immediate and personal.

“This is incredible!” I exclaimed, my voice barely above a whisper. The visitor beside me shared a knowing smile, reflecting the shared understanding that we were witnessing something profound. The intensity of the experience resonated deeply, and I left the deck with a renewed appreciation for the courage and resilience of those who lived through such harrowing times.

One of the highlights of my visit was the Space Shuttle Pavilion, housing the Enterprise. Standing beneath the massive shuttle, I felt a surge of awe and wonder. "Can you believe this?" I said to myself, marveling at the intersection of naval and space exploration. The exhibit chronicled the Intrepid's role in the Space Race, and I felt honored to witness this remarkable chapter of history.

Despite the earlier mishap with my phone, I managed to capture stunning photos and videos of the exhibits. Each snapshot became a portal to the past, a way to share this awe-inspiring experience with friends and family back home. I couldn't wait to tell them about the incredible stories and sights I had encountered.

As I delved deeper into the history of the USS Intrepid, I found myself completely captivated. The tales of bravery, innovation, and resilience were incredibly moving. My interest in history, once dormant, had been ignited. After leaving the museum, I eagerly downloaded every World War II documentary I could find, excited to learn more about the events that shaped our world.

This visit to the USS Intrepid was more than just a tour; it was a transformative journey. The ship, with its storied past and heroic legacy, had turned a history skeptic into a passionate enthusiast. "Travel really does change your perspective," I mused, reflecting on the day. The USS

Intrepid Museum wasn't just a highlight of my New York visit; it was an unforgettable experience that deepened my appreciation for history and the enduring spirit of those who lived it.

CHAPTER VIII

A Transformative Adventure: My First Trip to London

In 2012, I embarked on my first trip to London, a journey that would become a treasure trove of memories and lessons. The primary purpose of my trip was to attend a training session in Leicester, a charming city in England's East Midlands region. But before heading to Leicester, I decided to visit my college friend Jyotish, who was working in Birmingham at the time. Jyotish was as excited as I was about the trip and suggested I spend a day in Birmingham. He promised to take a day off to show me around the city.

I landed in Birmingham in the evening and checked into my hotel, already feeling the excitement of being in a new country. The next morning, Jyotish arrived to pick me up. He suggested I check out of the hotel since I would need to travel to Leicester later that day. We spent the entire day exploring Birmingham, and it was a delightful experience. We visited iconic landmarks and reminisced about our college days, laughing and sharing stories.

During our college years, we often drank Old Port Rum, a cheap but terrible-tasting drink that we'd gulp down in one shot while holding our noses to avoid the taste. So, when Jyotish handed me a glass of Jack Daniel's whiskey, I instinctively downed it in one go, just like the Old Port Rum. Jyotish burst out laughing. "Throw away your Kerala way of drinking!" he exclaimed. He then patiently taught me how to drink whiskey properly, savoring it sip by sip. It was a hilarious moment, and I couldn't help but laugh at my own naivety.

We left our baggage at the railway station's cloakroom, a concept entirely new to me, before heading out for the day. In the evening, Jyotish dropped me off at the railway station and helped me catch a train to Leicester. I arrived in Leicester around 7:30 PM and checked into a small family-run hotel near the railway station. The station was quite small and not very crowded. I called the hotel for directions and took a taxi to get there.

The next morning, I went to the hotel's restaurant for the complimentary breakfast included with my stay. The lady who owned the hotel, along with her family, greeted me warmly and asked about my sleep and my plans for the day. Their friendliness was a pleasant surprise, as it wasn't common practice where I came from. After breakfast, I asked for directions to the Institution of Occupational Safety and Health, where I had a one-day training session to become an instructor for IOSH courses. The lady suggested I walk, as it was only a 15-20 minute walk, and the weather was beautiful. She even drew me a map since GPS wasn't popular then.

Walking through the charming, green streets of Leicester was an absolute delight. The fresh air, coupled with the lush greenery, was invigorating and refreshing. As I strolled along, I noticed many locals walking their dogs. To my surprise and immense pleasure, almost everyone I passed smiled warmly and greeted me with a cheerful "good morning." This consistent friendliness was a new and delightful experience for me, coming from a place where such greetings from strangers were uncommon.

The genuine warmth and openness of the people I encountered in Leicester had a profound impact on me. It showcased a beautiful aspect of their culture—one where friendliness and cordial greetings were a norm rather than an exception. This simple yet powerful gesture of acknowledging others with a smile and a greeting filled me with positive energy and made me feel welcomed and valued, even as a visitor from a far-off land.

By the time I reached the training location, I was brimming with positive energy, buoyed by the kindness and friendliness of the people I had met along the way. This experience left a lasting impression on me, inspiring me to adopt this practice in my own life. I realized the profound effect a simple greeting could have on someone's day and resolved to carry this newfound habit back home. From then on, I made a conscious effort to greet people with a smile and a "good morning," hoping to spread the same warmth and positivity I had experienced in Leicester.

The training session was enlightening. I was the only participant from outside the UK, which made it a unique learning experience. Everyone was curious about my plans and my impressions of the UK. I mentioned that I was planning to go to London the next day and stay for two days before returning to Riyadh. One of the participants, a safety manager at Heathrow Airport, offered to drop me off at Heathrow and help me catch a train to London. I had already booked accommodation in Leicester for that night, but he assured me that the hotel would refund my money.

After the training, the gentleman I had met, who was a safety manager at Heathrow Airport, offered to help me with my travel arrangements. This unexpected kindness from someone I had just met that day took me by surprise. He drove me back to my hotel, and instead of just dropping me off, he came inside and spoke to the hotel staff. His demeanor was polite yet firm, and he managed to convince them to refund my money for the night's stay. I was truly impressed by his willingness to help and his effectiveness in resolving the situation.

He then drove me to Heathrow, a journey during which we chatted about various things, further cementing my appreciation for his kindness. Upon arriving at the airport, he didn't just leave me to figure things out on my own. Instead, he walked with me to the ticket counter, helped me purchase a train ticket, and made sure I was set for the next leg of my journey. His actions were a testament to the kindness and generosity of people, qualities I had not expected to encounter so strongly.

As I boarded the train and headed towards King's Cross Station in London, I reflected on this gentleman's extraordinary helpfulness. It struck me that he had gone out of his way to assist me, a complete stranger, ensuring that I could make the best out of my trip. His actions challenged my preconceived notions, shaped largely by movies and stories, that people in big cities could be indifferent or unkind. Instead, he showed me that kindness and generosity could be found everywhere.

Arriving at King's Cross Station, I was filled with a renewed sense of excitement and optimism for my adventure in London. However, little did I know, the most challenging part of my trip was just beginning. Despite the positive energy from the earlier encounter, I soon faced the daunting task of finding accommodation in a city teeming with visitors for a major event, which tested my patience and perseverance. But the memory of the gentleman's kindness kept my spirits high, reminding me of the goodness that exists in people, even in the most unexpected places..

Stepping off the train at King's Cross, I was immediately struck by the hustle and bustle of London. People were rushing around, and the energy of the city was palpable. With my heavy backpack weighing me down, I began my search for a hotel. I had read that it was possible to find decent accommodation for less than £100, so I was optimistic.

However, as I went from hotel to hotel, my optimism began to wane. Each receptionist I spoke to shook their head apologetically. "Fully booked," they would say. There was some kind of event in the city, and it seemed every hotel room in London was occupied.

The search quickly became a test of endurance. My shoulders started to ache from the weight of my backpack, and my feet were sore from walking. The city that had initially seemed so exciting now felt like an unforgiving maze. As the hours ticked by, my phone battery dwindled, adding to my sense of urgency. I needed to find a place before I was completely cut off from any help or directions.

Finally, after what felt like an eternity of walking and rejection, I stumbled upon a hotel that had a room available. My relief was short-lived when I was told the price was £200. It was well beyond my budget, so I declined and continued my search, though my hope was fading fast.

As the clock approached 9 PM, my situation became dire. My shoulders were burning, and to my dismay, I noticed blood stains on my shirt where the backpack straps had rubbed against my skin. Exhausted and nearly defeated, I walked into yet another hotel. The receptionist, who looked Indian, listened sympathetically as I explained my plight. "Sir, you should have booked in advance," he said. I nodded wearily, knowing he was right but needing help more than a lecture.

Seeing my desperation, he made a few phone calls. "There's a small room across the street," he said. "It's £100, but it's very basic." I didn't care about the size or the amenities; I just needed a place to sleep. I thanked him profusely and headed to the hotel he recommended.

When I finally arrived at the last available hotel, exhausted and desperate, the receptionist led me to a room that was, quite literally, a last resort. The room was tucked under a narrow staircase, with a slanting ceiling that made it impossible to stand upright except in one corner. It felt like a scene out of a Dickens novel. The room was dimly lit, and the single small window barely let in any light. The walls seemed to close in on me, amplifying the claustrophobic feeling.

The bed was comically small for my six-foot frame, more suited for a child than an adult. I had to pull a chair to the foot of the bed to support my legs, creating a makeshift extension. The chair creaked ominously every time I shifted, adding to the surreal nature of the situation. I could almost hear my back groaning in sympathy with the chair as I tried to find a comfortable position.

The bathroom was no better. It was so tiny that I could barely move without bumping into the walls. Showering required me to keep my arms tightly against my sides, making me feel like I was trapped in a phone booth. The water pressure was weak, and the temperature fluctuated unpredictably, from scalding hot to icy cold. Despite all this, I couldn't help but laugh at the absurdity of it all. The stark contrast to my expectations was almost comical.

But at that moment, despite the cramped conditions and the almost farcical nature of the room, it felt like heaven. After hours of wandering the streets of London with a heavy backpack, my shoulders aching and my feet sore, I was just grateful to have a roof over my head and a place to rest. The thought of sleeping on the streets had been a real possibility, and this tiny room, with all its imperfections, was a sanctuary.

As I lay there, half my body on the bed and half on the chair, I felt a wave of relief wash over me. The bed might have been small and the room claustrophobic, but it was mine for the night. The hum of the city outside became a soothing lullaby, and the room, with all its quirks, turned into a safe haven. This unexpected twist in my journey had taught me the value of gratitude and resilience, and I drifted off to sleep with a newfound appreciation for the little things in life.

That night, as I lay in the cramped bed with my legs propped up on a chair, I reflected on the day's events. It had been a grueling experience, but it taught me a valuable lesson: never travel without booking accommodation in advance. The next two days in London were fantastic. I explored the city on a hop-on-hop-off bus, visiting Buckingham Palace, the Tower of London, Big Ben, and taking a ride on the London Eye. Each landmark left me in awe, and I soaked in the rich history and vibrant culture of the city.

Looking back, my first trip to London was an exciting and eye-opening adventure that I'll always cherish. It was filled with laughter, new experiences, and valuable lessons. Since then, I've returned to London eight times, each visit bringing new adventures and memories. But that first trip, with all its trials and triumphs, will always hold a special place in my heart.

Reflecting on the journey, I remember the thrill of exploring Birmingham with Jyotish, the hilarity of my first sip of Jack Daniel's, and the warmth of the people in Leicester who transformed a routine walk into a heartwarming experience. The simple greetings from strangers filled me with positive energy and taught me the beauty of kindness and openness. It was a cultural revelation that changed the way I interacted with people, instilling in me the habit of greeting others with a smile and a "good morning."

Then, there was the incredible kindness of the gentleman from my training, who went above and beyond to help a stranger. His actions challenged my preconceived notions about big city indifference, showing me that generosity and kindness exist everywhere, even in the most unexpected places. His help not only made my journey smoother but also left a lasting impression on me about the inherent goodness in people.

The climax of my adventure came with the frantic search for a hotel room in London, which tested my endurance and resolve. The room I finally found, cramped and tucked under a staircase, felt like a haven despite its shortcomings. It was a humbling experience that taught me the value of gratitude and the importance of being adaptable and resilient in the face of challenges.

Every moment of that trip, from the laughter shared with friends to the kindness of strangers and the lessons learned through adversity, shaped me in profound ways. Each subsequent visit to London has been wonderful, but none have matched the sheer emotional depth and transformative impact of that first trip.

It was more than just a visit to a new city; it was a journey of personal growth and discovery. The trials and triumphs of that trip became foundational memories that I carry with me, reminding me of the joy of exploration, the warmth of human connection, and the strength found in overcoming challenges. That first trip to London will always hold a special place in my heart, a reminder of the adventure, the lessons, and the beautiful unpredictability of life.

CHAPTER IX

Lisbon Magic: Exploring History, Culture, and Custard Tarts

Our trip to Lisbon was a perfect mix of family bonding, cultural exploration, and culinary indulgence. We spent four unforgettable days in this beautiful, historic city, with its charming, narrow streets, iconic trams, and steep hills that tested both our legs and our curiosity.

We had booked a lovely four-bedroom apartment through Airbnb, located in one of Lisbon's older neighborhoods. The apartment had an old-world charm that captivated us the moment we stepped in. From the vintage décor to the stunning hand showers in the bathrooms, it was unlike anything we had experienced in European accommodations before. The apartment had a homey, warm atmosphere, and we enjoyed cooking dinners and breakfasts together. Nandhu, our friend who had joined us with his family, turned out to be an excellent cook, treating us to delicious meals in the cozy kitchen. Conveniently, there was a small grocery shop nearby, run by a friendly Nepalese family, where we bought fresh ingredients and essentials every day.

Lisbon, with its endless steep streets, is a city of contrasts—where modernity blends effortlessly with its rich historical legacy. Walking through the city felt like stepping back in time. The cobblestone streets, colorful tiles, and classic trams added a layer of romance to every corner we explored. But these picturesque streets also came with a challenge—the steep hills that seemed to pop up everywhere! Each climb, however, rewarded us with stunning views of the city below, the winding Tagus River, and Lisbon's iconic red rooftops.

The vibrancy of Lisbon was infectious. Whether it was the street musicians filling the air with the soulful sounds of Fado, the bustling squares, or the aroma of freshly baked pastries wafting from every corner bakery, Lisbon invited us to slow down and savor its charm.

Our trip to Lisbon took an unexpected turn when we decided to hire a guide through the Showaround app. That's how we met Violet, a vibrant and friendly Ukrainian girl who had found herself in Lisbon, unable to return to her homeland due to the ongoing conflict. Despite her challenges, Violet's energy and warmth were contagious, and we knew right away that she would be the perfect companion for our Lisbon adventure.

We arranged to meet at Rossio Square, one of the city's most iconic and bustling spots. The air buzzed with the sounds of chatter and street performers, and the grandeur of the surrounding buildings made it a postcard-worthy setting to start our tour. We arrived a little early and, naturally, couldn't resist the lure of a nearby bakery selling Portugal's famed custard tarts—Pastel de Nata. Having read about these delicacies long before the trip, we eagerly dove into our first bite, and it was everything we had imagined: creamy, flaky perfection.

Just as we were finishing up, Violet arrived, her smile as bright as the Lisbon sunshine. But when she saw us with crumbs of Pastel de Nata on our lips, her eyes widened in playful shock. "No, no, no!" she exclaimed, laughing. "I was saving the best Pastel de Nata in Lisbon for you! This one," she gestured at our pastries, "is just the appetizer." Her good-natured teasing set the tone for what would become an unforgettable day.

"Don't worry," she winked, "I know the place where these tarts will make you forget all about the ones you've just had." Intrigued, and now with our expectations sky-high, we followed Violet deeper into the city, eager to discover what hidden gem she had up her sleeve. The tour had just begun, and already, Lisbon had started to weave its magic on us—thanks to Violet's infectious enthusiasm.

Later in the day, Violet kept her promise and took us to *Pastéis de Bacalhau,* tucked inside the beautiful *Casa Portuguesa do Pastel de Bacalhau.* As we approached, she grinned and said, "This is where your *Pastel de Nata* experience gets completely overshadowed!" We laughed, knowing by now to trust her judgment.

The place was stunning, not just a regular bakery but more like a grand salon with ornate tiles and chandeliers hanging from high ceilings. "Welcome to one of Lisbon's hidden treasures," Violet said, motioning towards the towering *Santa Justa Elevator* next to the building. "This elevator is a masterpiece—designed by one of Gustave Eiffel's apprentices, actually."

As the elevator rose slowly, Lisbon unfolded before our eyes, a sea of red rooftops, winding cobblestone streets, and the glittering river stretching towards the horizon. "Isn't it breathtaking?" Violet asked, clearly enjoying our reactions. "Day or night, this view never fails to wow. But at dusk," she winked, "it gets even more romantic."

We reached the top, where the city seemed to stretch out endlessly below. "Wow," I said, not quite able to find the right words for the view. Violet just smiled knowingly. "Wait till you try what I have planned next," she teased.

Back at *Casa Portuguesa,* we took our seats, and Violet motioned for the server. The air was filled with the delicate chime of an ancient music box, adding a dreamy atmosphere to the place. "Do you hear that? This music box has been playing here for over a hundred years," she said. "Pretty magical, right?"

Then came the pièce de résistance: *Pastéis de Bacalhau*—golden codfish cakes with a decadent Serra cheese filling. "Now, take your time with this," Violet instructed as the server poured us each a glass of Port Wine. "These are no ordinary codfish cakes. They're legendary."

We each took a bite, and our eyes widened in delight. The crispy outer layer gave way to the rich, creamy cheese inside, perfectly complemented by the sweet, smooth taste of Port. "This is... unreal," my wife said, savoring each bite. Violet laughed. "Told you! Nothing like the snacks you had earlier, right?"

As we sat there, enjoying the food, the music, and the view, it felt like the perfect Lisbon moment. "So," Violet leaned in, "how does this stack up against your first *Pastel de Nata?*" I shook my head in mock defeat. "Alright, you win. This takes the cake—literally."

Before we left, something caught my eye: the beautifully designed Port Wine glasses. "You know," Violet smiled, "you can take one home. Consider it a little keepsake of our day together."

We couldn't resist. As we made our way back down the elevator, the glass safely tucked away in our bag, I turned to Violet. "Every time we use this at home, we'll remember today," I said. She smiled warmly. "That's the point. Lisbon has a way of staying with you."

One of the most interesting spots Violet took us to was *A Brasileira,* the oldest Brazilian coffee shop in Lisbon, where Portuguese intellectuals once gathered. Opened in 1905, this café still maintains its old-world charm, with ornate wooden interiors, brass fixtures, and a palpable sense of history. We enjoyed a cup of their famous *bica,* a strong Portuguese espresso, while soaking in the rich literary and artistic history of the place. It was a surreal experience to sit in a café where great writers like Fernando Pessoa once pondered over their works. The bronze statue of Pessoa sitting outside the café is a popular spot for tourists, and of course, we couldn't resist taking a photo with the literary legend.

No trip to Lisbon is truly complete without standing in the shadow of the awe-inspiring Mosteiro dos Jerónimos (Jerónimos Monastery), a UNESCO World Heritage site that practically demands your attention. It's like it knows it's the grand jewel of the Age of Discovery, and let's be honest—it is. This 16th-century masterpiece of Manueline architecture has a way of making you feel like you're walking through a living history book... which is ironic because, back in the day, I hated history.

Yes, I admit it. In school, history and I were not friends. Memorizing dates, names, and battles? I'd rather have watched paint dry! Vasco da Gama? Just another name to scribble down before the bell rang. Fast forward to the present, and here I am, voluntarily visiting the tomb of Vasco da Gama—the very guy whose sea route to Kerala, my home state, was nothing more than a paragraph in my history textbook. And to top it off, I'm actually enjoying it! Who would've thought?

But the real historian in our family is my wife. She used to teach history and, let me tell you, her excitement levels were through the roof. "Can you believe it? Vasco da Gama! In Kerala, our backyard! And now we're standing by his tomb!" she said, her voice nearly trembling with joy. I half-expected her to start giving a full-blown lecture right there in the monastery.

While I was absorbing the significance of the moment (and, let's be honest, trying not to look too lost), she was pointing out every little detail of the Manueline carvings like a kid in a candy store. "Look at this craftsmanship! It's like a stone version of Portugal's greatest hits!" she exclaimed. I nodded along, thinking, *Wow, I've come a long way from dreading history class to now having a personal guide who's THIS passionate about it.*

And then there was the food! Our guide, Violet, smiled knowingly as she shared the monastery's sweetest secret—the origin of the Pastel de Nata. "The monks created these to support the monastery," she said. "Not a bad way to make history, huh?" My wife, naturally, tied it all back to the lesson. "This is how history should be taught," she said, grinning as she bit into the custard tart. "Not just facts, but with stories, places, and food!"

I couldn't argue with that. Maybe history wasn't so bad after all—especially if it came with a side of Pastel de Nata.

Our four days in Lisbon were a perfect mix of adventure, culture, and food, all made unforgettable by the city's charm and our amazing guide, Violet. Lisbon's steep streets tested our endurance but rewarded us with stunning views of its iconic red rooftops and the Tagus River. We indulged in *Pastel de Nata* at every corner, but Violet introduced us to the best spots, adding fun and flavor to the experience.

The city's history, which I once found dull in school, came alive when we visited the tomb of Vasco da Gama. My wife, a former history teacher, was over the moon with excitement, and to my surprise, our 8th standard son shared that enthusiasm. He was thrilled to see in person what he had learned in his textbooks, making the experience even more special. Lisbon's warmth, beauty, and delicious food made it a place we'll always remember, and we're already dreaming of returning one day.

CHAPTER X

Madrid: Where Adventure Meets Culture

We embarked on our journey from Lisbon to Madrid via FlixBus, a comfortable yet exciting ride that promised new adventures. Along the way, we made a stop for food, and that's when I was eager to put my recently acquired Spanish skills to the test. After a month of learning on the Preply app, with guidance from my native teacher from Madrid, I felt confident enough to navigate the language in real-life situations.

Before the trip, my teacher had provided me with invaluable tips—everything from essential phrases for traveling to must-visit places and the most delicious local dishes. Armed with this knowledge and a list of recommendations, I felt ready for the adventure ahead.

One of the reasons I took learning Spanish so seriously was my wife's food allergies. She's allergic to ingredients like mushrooms and broccoli, which can easily be overlooked when ordering food abroad. So, I made it a point to learn how to communicate her allergies clearly in Spanish. This turned out to be incredibly useful as we ordered food during the stop. I confidently explained her dietary restrictions to the staff, who quickly adjusted her order without any confusion. It was a relief knowing we could safely enjoy local cuisine without the worry of triggering an allergic reaction.

As we continued our journey to Madrid, I felt a deep sense of accomplishment—not just for learning a new language but for using it in a way that truly mattered. It added an extra layer of connection to the culture, and I was excited for what the rest of our trip had in store.

As we settled into our seats, I noticed a Bangladeshi couple nearby, wrangling their energetic toddler who seemed determined to explore every nook of the bus.

The father caught my eye and offered an apologetic smile. "I hope he doesn't disturb your sleep too much," he said as I settled into my aisle seat.

I chuckled. "No worries! I'm just hoping to catch a few winks."

But, as luck would have it, their little boy had other plans. Every fifteen minutes, he'd pop out of his seat, wandering down the aisle, turning my attempts at sleep into a comedy of interruptions. After a few rounds of this, I couldn't help but smile, and curiosity got the better of me. I struck up a conversation with the father, who was trying to calm his restless son.

He spoke to me in Hindi, which immediately broke the ice. "I used to work in Saudi Arabia," he said, leaning in a little closer so as not to wake his wife, who was finally getting some rest. "I made sandwiches there. Bought a visa for a hefty price and moved to Paris."

I nodded, intrigued. "Wow, that's quite the journey."

He smiled. "My wife joined me later, and we've been in Paris ever since. Our son was born there."

"That's amazing! So, are you heading to Madrid for a holiday?" I asked, figuring they were fellow travelers on a similar adventure.

He shook his head. "No, we're actually heading back to Paris. This bus stops in Madrid, but we just came from Lisbon. We were there to get my son's European passport. In a few years, we'll get ours too."

"That's incredible," I said, impressed by how far they had come, both literally and figuratively.

As we spoke, I couldn't help but think how borders were starting to blur, and how stories like theirs were becoming more common. "The world is really becoming one big community, isn't it?" I mused with a hopeful smile.

He nodded, his eyes bright with optimism. "Yes, soon there won't be any differences—just people, living and working together."

It was a simple bus ride, but it felt like a glimpse into the future—a world where cultures mix, and connections transcend borders.

We had booked a hotel in Madrid through Airbnb, thinking we found the perfect spot for our stay. But as soon as we arrived, we realized the mistake we'd made. There we were—four adults, three kids, and a pile of seven heavy bags—standing in front of a two-bedroom flat that seemed much smaller in person than it did in the photos.

As I looked up, I spotted the real kicker: the flat was on the second floor, with no elevator in sight.

"This... is going to be interesting," I muttered, already feeling the weight of the bags on my shoulders.

My wife glanced at the stairs, eyes widening. "Wait, how are we supposed to lug all this up? And there's only one toilet?"

"One toilet for seven people?" my friend Nandhu asked, half-laughing, half in disbelief.

"It's like a scene from a bad movie," I joked, trying to keep the mood light, though the reality of our situation was starting to sink in.

The kids, completely oblivious, were already racing up the stairs, while the adults stood there, exchanging helpless looks.

"Alright, let's get this over with," Nandhu, grabbing the first of the heavy bags.

Each step felt like a challenge, and by the time we managed to get everything up to the second floor, we were all exhausted.

"This is going to be a long stay," my wife said, leaning against the doorframe.

I chuckled, though I could feel the tension in my back from carrying the bags. "At least we're getting a workout." But deep down, we all knew—it was going to be a long couple of days in that cramped little flat.

The next day, we decided to explore Madrid with the help of a local guide. I had booked Ivanka through the Showaround app, and as soon as we met her, I knew we were in for a fun day.

"Ready to see the real Madrid?" she asked with a smile.

"Absolutely! Lead the way!" I replied, and off we went.

Our first stop was Puerta del Sol, one of the busiest squares in the city. As we stood there, Ivanka pointed to a small plaque on the ground. "This is Kilometre Zero," she explained. "All roads in Spain are measured from this very spot."

The kids were fascinated, and we took a few photos, trying to capture the moment.

After visiting Kilometre Zero, Ivanka led us to one of Madrid's most iconic food destinations—the **Mercado de San Miguel**. As soon as we walked in, the vibrant atmosphere of the market hit us—buzzing with locals and tourists alike, all drawn to the colorful stalls packed with mouth-watering delicacies.

"This place is a food lover's paradise," Ivanka said with a grin, gesturing toward the array of stalls. "Here, you can taste the best of Spain, all in one spot."

We started by tasting **mussels**, which were fresh, briny, and perfectly seasoned. "These are amazing," I said, impressed by the simplicity and the flavor. But that was just the beginning.

At another stall, we tried **jamón ibérico**—the famous Iberian ham that melts in your mouth. "You haven't really tasted Spain until you've had this," Ivanka pointed out, and she was right. The rich, slightly nutty flavor of the ham paired with a crisp piece of bread was a revelation.

Next up was **croquetas**, golden and crispy on the outside, with a creamy béchamel and ham filling inside. The kids devoured them in no time, and even I couldn't resist going back for seconds.

"Try the **tortilla de patatas**," Ivanka suggested at the next stall. We were served a thick slice of Spanish omelet, filled with layers of soft potatoes and onions. "This is classic comfort food," I said, taking a bite and loving the balance of textures.

We then moved on to **paella**, and the saffron-scented rice, loaded with seafood and chicken, was a feast for both the eyes and the taste buds. "I could eat this every day," my wife said, clearly delighted.

For dessert, Ivanka insisted we try the **tarta de Santiago**, an almond cake that was light, moist, and dusted with powdered sugar. "It's a traditional dessert from Galicia," she explained, "and one of my favorites." By the looks of my plate, it quickly became one of mine too.

By the time we left the market, we were stuffed but satisfied. "Mercado de San Miguel is like a mini culinary tour of Spain," I said, reflecting on the incredible variety of foods we'd tried.

Ivanka nodded, smiling. "That's what makes it special—there's always something new to discover here."

It was an unforgettable food journey, and I knew this market would be one of the highlights of our trip to Madrid.

After our food tour, we headed to the Prado Museum, one of the most renowned art museums in the world. "The Prado is famous for its collection of European masterpieces," Ivanka explained as we wandered through the halls, marveling at the works of Goya and Velázquez. "But trust me, even if you're not an art lover, it's worth a visit."

Finally, we made our way to Plaza Mayor, where the kids had a blast. As we walked through the grand square, a man dressed as a hilariously oversized Spider-Man caught their attention.

"Look, it's Spider-Man!" my son shouted, running toward him with wide eyes.

The kids were over the moon, taking pictures and high-fiving the "fat" Spider-Man while he posed dramatically for them.

By the end of the day, we were exhausted but happy, grateful for Ivanka's expertise and her fun, lighthearted way of showing us the city. As we wrapped up, she smiled and said, "Hope you enjoyed the tour!"

"Absolutely," I grinned. "You showed us so much of Madrid in just one day. Thank you for everything."

She winked, "It was my pleasure. Enjoy the rest of your stay in this beautiful city!"

With that, we said our goodbyes, thankful for the memories she helped create during our whirlwind tour of Madrid.

The next day was Sunday, and my Preply teacher had excitedly told me about Madrid's famous **El Rastro**—the bustling Sunday market that's a must-visit for anyone in the city. "It's one of the largest flea markets in Europe," she had said, "and you'll find everything there—from antiques to quirky souvenirs, clothes, and even street performances. It's a mix of culture, history, and shopping all in one place."

Intrigued by her description, we decided to explore it ourselves. Set in the La Latina neighborhood, El Rastro spans several streets, and the atmosphere was electric the moment we arrived. Stalls stretched endlessly, selling everything you could imagine—handmade jewelry, vintage clothes, art pieces, old books, and even antiques with rich stories behind them. It was as much about the experience as it was about the shopping.

"Wow, this place is massive!" my wife exclaimed as we wove through the crowd.

"You're going to love this," I replied, remembering how my teacher had raved about the unique finds hidden among the stalls.

As we walked, vendors called out to passersby, enticing us with their treasures. The kids were mesmerized by the eclectic mix of goods, from vibrant scarves to old vinyl records and quirky trinkets. At one point, we stumbled upon a stall selling vintage cameras, and I couldn't resist stopping to admire the collection.

The market wasn't just about shopping; it was alive with the energy of street performers, local food vendors, and the chatter of both locals and tourists. We stopped for **bocadillos de calamares**—fried squid sandwiches, a classic Madrid snack, recommended by my teacher. "You have to try this!" I said, handing one to my wife. The crispy calamari paired with fresh bread was the perfect mid-morning treat.

As we continued through the market, we stumbled upon a group of street musicians performing in the middle of the bustling crowd. They were strumming guitars and singing what seemed like a Spanish hit song. The energy was contagious—people around us began to join in, clapping and singing along as if it were a neighborhood anthem.

We didn't understand a word of the lyrics, but it didn't matter. The rhythm, the vibe, and the pure joy in the air pulled us in. My wife and I exchanged smiles as the kids started moving to the beat, soaking up the infectious energy of the moment. It was one of those spontaneous experiences that made us feel connected to the city, even without speaking the language.

"Whatever this song is, I love it!" I said, laughing as the crowd sang louder, completely immersed in the performance.

The music echoed through the market, adding a layer of magic to an already vibrant day. Even though we couldn't sing along, we enjoyed every note, carried away by the rhythm and the energy of Madrid.

We strolled through the colorful maze of stalls, I understood why my Preply teacher was so fond of El Rastro. It was more than just a market—it was a vibrant celebration of Madrid's culture, and every corner held a new surprise.

That night, we decided to immerse ourselves in one of Spain's most iconic cultural experiences—**flamenco.** After hearing so much about its passionate energy and dramatic flair, we couldn't leave Madrid without seeing a live performance.

We arrived at a traditional **tablao**—a small, intimate venue designed specifically for flamenco shows. The dim lighting and rustic décor created the perfect atmosphere for what we were about to witness. As we took our seats near the stage, there was a sense of anticipation in the air, the soft strumming of a guitar filling the room.

When the performance began, the room fell silent. The dancers emerged, their vibrant costumes catching the light as they moved with intensity and grace. The singer's deep, soulful voice echoed through the space, telling a story we couldn't understand, but the emotion was clear. The rhythm of the **palmas** (hand clapping) and the intricate guitar melodies accompanied every step, every stomp of the dancers' feet. It was a mesmerizing display of passion and artistry.

I leaned over to my wife, whispering, "I've never seen anything like this. The energy is unbelievable."

She nodded, her eyes fixed on the stage, captivated by the raw emotion in every movement.

The highlight of the night was the **baile**, where the lead dancer took center stage. Her movements were fierce and precise, her feet pounding the floor in perfect sync with the rapid claps and strums of the guitar. The crowd was transfixed, and you could feel the intensity build with each step, each spin, as if the room itself was breathing in time with the music.

By the end of the performance, the room erupted in applause, but we were left in awe, still processing the beauty of what we had just witnessed. It wasn't just a dance—it was a story, a celebration of Spanish culture, and a window into the soul of flamenco. We left the **tablao** that night with our hearts full, grateful to have experienced such an unforgettable piece of Madrid's vibrant spirit.

The next day, we made our way to **Las Rozas Village**, known as the best outlet shopping destination in Madrid. It's a bit of a tradition for us to visit outlet malls whenever we travel, and Las Rozas didn't disappoint—it's like a small, luxury village dedicated entirely to shopping. We've found that the prices at outlets are always much better than regular stores, so we were excited to see what we could find.

As we arrived, we were greeted by the charming, open-air setup, with beautifully designed boutiques lining the streets. The place had a relaxed yet sophisticated vibe, with well-known brands offering incredible discounts. From high-end fashion to accessories and even home goods, Las Rozas Village had it all.

"This is going to be dangerous for my wallet," I joked, as we started browsing the stores.

My wife was immediately drawn to a few designer boutiques, while I scouted out some great deals on clothing and shoes. The kids were happy to tag along, enjoying the open space and the occasional ice cream break between shops. We wandered in and out of stores, picking up a few items we had been eyeing, and discovering some unexpected bargains along the way.

"What I love about these outlet malls," my wife said, "is that you can get quality brands for a fraction of the price."

"Exactly," I agreed, admiring a new jacket I had just bought at a steep discount. "It's like a treasure hunt—you never know what you're going to find."

After a few hours of shopping, our bags were full, and we felt satisfied with our haul. The great deals made it worth the trip, and the experience itself was a lot more relaxed compared to the hustle of regular city shopping.

Las Rozas Village turned out to be one of the highlights of our trip for its mix of luxury, convenience, and unbeatable prices. It's definitely a must-visit for any shopper passing through Madrid!

As our time in Madrid came to an end, I couldn't help but reflect on the incredible journey we had experienced. From the vibrant streets of El Rastro to the passionate flamenco performances, from the bustling food stalls of Mercado de San Miguel to the calm luxury of Las Rozas Village, Madrid had revealed itself as a city of contrasts—where tradition and modernity dance together in perfect harmony.

What made this trip truly special, though, were the connections we made along the way. Whether it was bonding over shared experiences with fellow travelers on a bus, navigating language barriers to ensure my wife's safety with her food allergies, or laughing with our guide Ivanka as she showed us her beloved city, Madrid wasn't just a place—it was an experience that opened doors to new friendships and insights. It taught us that travel isn't just about visiting new places but about how those places transform you.

As we prepared to leave, I felt a deep sense of gratitude for the cultural immersion we'd had and the memories we created as a family. Madrid had given us a tapestry of experiences, rich with color, flavor, and emotion. It's a city that makes you feel alive, that invites you to step out of your comfort zone, and that rewards you with moments of unexpected joy and connection.

With one last look at the vibrant cityscape before heading to our next destination, I knew that Madrid had left an indelible mark on our hearts. This wasn't just a trip—it was a reminder of how vast and beautiful the world is, and how every adventure, no matter how planned or spontaneous, leaves you with stories to cherish for a lifetime.

Until next time, Madrid. You'll always be a part of our story.

Acknowledgments

I would like to express my deepest gratitude to the key people who inspired and helped me throughout the process of writing and publishing this work.

First and foremost, I am profoundly thankful to my wife, Soumia, for all her unwavering support. Her encouragement and belief in me have been the bedrock of this journey. To our kids, Sreeram and Durga, thank you for bringing joy and balance into my life, allowing me to pursue my passion.

I am forever indebted to my mother, Sarojiniamma, whose strength and love have been my guiding light. My late father, Ramakrishna Pillai, who always wanted me to reach the top, remains my greatest inspiration. My sisters, Manju and Mini, have been my pillars of support, always cheering me on.

A heartfelt thanks to my friend and former colleague, Mrs. Rita Sabu. Her motivation to publish this book, along with her invaluable suggestions and meticulous proofreading of each article, were crucial. She also helped me connect with fellow authors, expanding my horizons and enriching this journey.

I am deeply grateful to the writer, Mr. P. J. J. Anthony, for his guidance on how to publish my book. His expertise and advice have been instrumental in bringing this work to fruition.

Special thanks to my friend and colleague, Mr. Muath Alangari, a great traveler and companion during my travels to many countries. His camaraderie and shared experiences have significantly influenced the stories within this book.

Lastly, I extend my appreciation to all my friends and others who supported me along the way. Your encouragement and belief in my work have been invaluable.

To all of you, thank you from the bottom of my heart. This book would not have been possible without your support and inspiration.

www.ingramcontent.com/pod-product-compliance
Lightning Source LLC
LaVergne TN
LVHW041108150826
845673LV00007B/1974

* 9 7 9 8 8 9 5 8 8 6 1 2 0 *